DEINONYCHUS

A Buddy Book
by
Christy Devillier

ABDO
Publishing Company

VISIT US AT
www.abdopub.com

Published by ABDO Publishing Company, 4940 Viking Drive, Edina, Minnesota 55435. Copyright © 2004 by Abdo Consulting Group, Inc. International copyrights reserved in all countries. No part of this book may be reproduced in any form without written permission from the publisher.

Printed in the United States.

Edited by: Michael P. Goecke
Contributing Editor: Matt Ray
Graphic Design: Denise Esner, Maria Hosley
Image Research: Deborah Coldiron
Illustrations: Deborah Coldiron, Denise Esner, Maria Hosley
Photographs: Corel, Hulton Archives, Imagelibrary, Minden Pictures

Library of Congress Cataloging-in-Publication Data

Devillier, Christy, 1971-
    Deinonychus/Christy Devillier.
        p. cm. -- (Dinosaurs)
    Includes index.
    Summary: Describes the physical characteristics, habitat, and behavior of a small but fast and deadly dinosaur, the Deinonychus.
    ISBN 1-59197-538-7
    1. Deinonychus—Juvenile literature. [1. Deinonychus. 2. Dinosaurs.] I. Title.

QE862.S3D476 2004
567.912—dc22
                                                    2003057818

TABLE OF CONTENTS

WHAT WERE THEY?

The Deinonychus was a fast and deadly dinosaur. It had sharp teeth and claws. The Deinonychus lived about 100 million years ago.

Deinonychus
Dy-NON-ik-uss

The Deinonychus was about
as heavy as a person.

The Deinonychus was about 10 feet (three m) long. It stood about five feet (two m) tall. The Deinonychus weighed around 150 pounds (68 kg). This is as heavy as a person.

TAIL

Scientists believe the Deinonychus was a fast runner. This dinosaur ran on its two back legs. It had four clawed toes on its feet. The claw on its second toe was bigger than the others. The Deinonychus lifted its second toe off the ground as it walked or ran.

MOUTH

ARM

LEG

FOOT

7

The Deinonychus had long arms and strong hands. It could grab with its hands. Each hand had three clawed fingers.

The Deinonychus had bony rods in its tail. These rods made its tail very stiff. A stiff tail may have helped the Deinonychus make quick turns. The tail probably helped with balance, too.

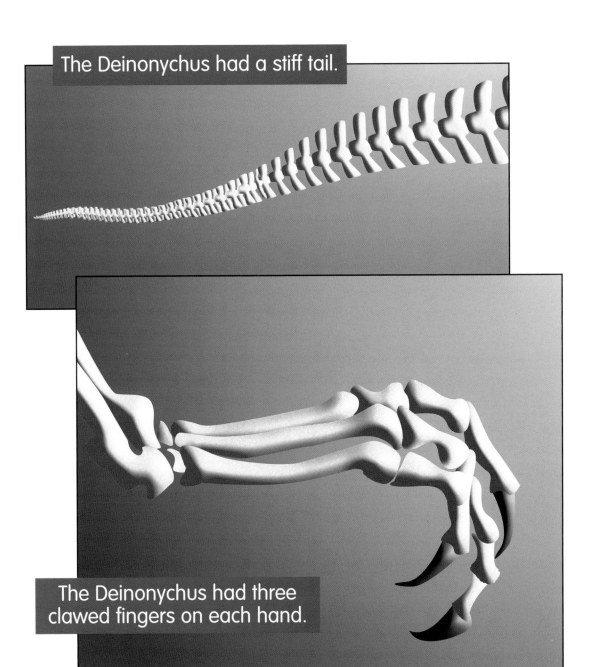

The Deinonychus had a stiff tail.

The Deinonychus had three clawed fingers on each hand.

The Deinonychus's name means "terrible claw." Scientists named the Deinonychus after its biggest foot claw. This "terrible claw" was on the second toe of each foot. Scientists believe the Deinonychus used these big claws to kill prey.

The Deinonychus probably killed prey with its "terrible claw."

WHERE DID THEY LIVE?

The Deinonychus lived in western North America. It lived on land that is now Montana, Utah, and Wyoming. Back then, a shallow sea covered much of North America. It was called the Colorado Sea. The Deinonychus lived west of the Colorado Sea.

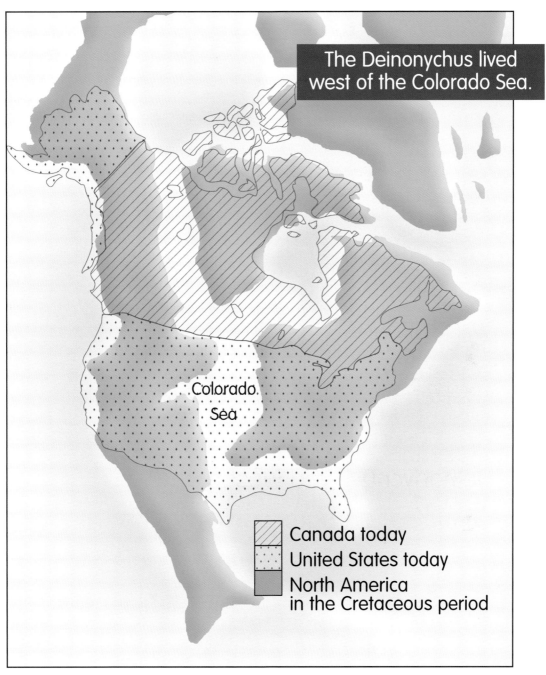

The Deinonychus lived west of the Colorado Sea.

Colorado Sea

Canada today
United States today
North America in the Cretaceous period

The Deinonychus lived during the Cretaceous period. Back then, the world was very different. The weather was tropical. Forests covered the land. The forests were full of evergreens, palm trees, horsetails, and tree ferns. There were flowering plants, too.

The Cretaceous world was full of tropical forests.

The Deinonychus lived among other animals. There were insects, such as ants and beetles. There were lizards and small, furry mammals, too. Back then, many mammals were as small as mice.

Ants, beetles, and other insects were around during the Cretaceous period.

17

Turtles, squid, crabs, and fish lived in the sea. Crocodiles and frogs lived in swamps. Seabirds flew in the skies. They had teeth for eating fish. One of these seabirds was the Ichthyornis. Its name means "fish-bird."

The Hesperornis was a bird that did not fly. It swam in the water and ate fish.

The Hesperornis was a swimming bird that ate fish.

The Deinonychus was a carnivore. Carnivores eat meat. The Deinonychus hunted other animals. It may have jumped onto its prey to kill it. The Deinonychus probably killed prey with its claws.

The Deinonychus most likely ate anything it could catch and kill. The Tenontosaurus was probably one of its prey.

The Deinonychus may have hunted the Tenontosaurus, a plant-eating dinosaur.

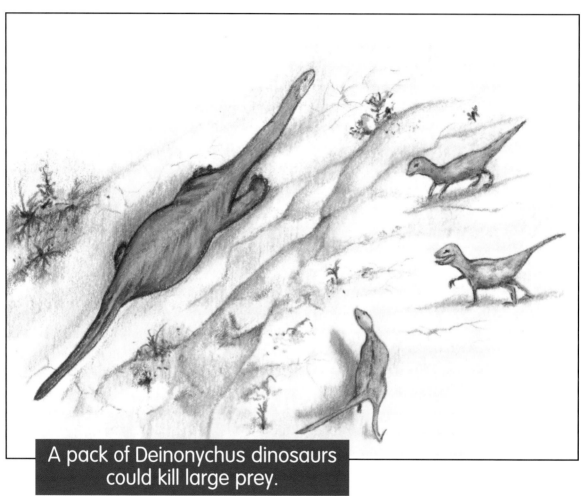

A pack of Deinonychus dinosaurs could kill large prey.

The Deinonychus may have hunted together at times. A pack of Deinonychus dinosaurs could kill bigger animals.

The Deinonychus could open its mouth very wide. It had a strong bite, too. Inside its mouth were many sharp, serrated teeth. Serrated teeth have tiny, sharp points along an edge. The Deinonychus's teeth pointed backward. This may have helped it tear and chew its food.

The Deinonychus belongs to the Dromaeosauridae family. Dromaeosaur dinosaurs were good hunters. Scientists believe they were among the smartest dinosaurs.

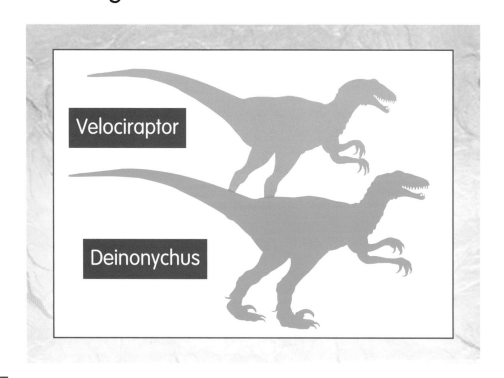

Velociraptor

Deinonychus

Another Dromaeosaur was the Velociraptor. It was one of the fastest dinosaurs. The Velociraptor could probably run about 40 miles (64 km) per hour. Like other Dromaeosaurs, it ran on its two back legs. The Velociraptor also had special killing claws.

Paleontologists study fossils. Barnum Brown was a famous paleontologist. He found fossils from a Dromaeosaur dinosaur in 1914. It was the first time anyone discovered a Dromaeosaur dinosaur.

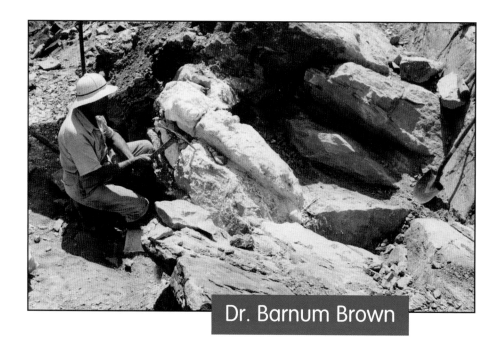

Dr. Barnum Brown

More fossils from a Dromaeosaur dinosaur were found in 1964. Grant Meyer and John Ostrom found them in Montana. Ostrom called the dinosaur Deinonychus antirrhopus. Over the years, people have found other Deinonychus fossils in Utah and Wyoming.

American Museum of Natural History
Central Park West at 79th Street
New York, NY 10024-5192
http://www.amnh.org/

Peabody Museum of Natural History
Yale University
170 Whitney Avenue
New Haven, CT 06520-8118
http://www.peabody.yale.edu/

DEINONYCHUS

NAME MEANS	Terrible claw
DIET	Meat
WEIGHT	150 pounds (68 kg)
HEIGHT	5 feet (2 m)
TIME	Cretaceous Period
ANOTHER DROMAEOSAUR	Velociraptor
SPECIAL FEATURE	Big claws
FOSSILS FOUND	USA— Montana, Utah, Wyoming

The Deinonychus lived 100 million years ago.

The first humans appeared 1.6 million years ago.

Triassic Period	Jurassic Period	Cretaceous Period	Tertiary Period
245 Million years ago	208 Million years ago	144 Million years ago	65 Million years ago
Mesozoic Era			Cenozoic Era

29

WEB SITES

To learn more about the Deinonychus, visit ABDO Publishing Company on the World Wide Web. Web sites about the Deinonychus are featured on our "Book Links" page. These links are routinely monitored and updated to provide the most current information available.

www.abdopub.com

IMPORTANT WORDS

carnivore a meat-eater.

Cretaceous period a period of time that happened 144–65 million years ago.

dinosaur reptiles that lived on land 248–65 million years ago.

fossil remains of very old animals and plants commonly found in the ground. A fossil can be a bone, a footprint, or any trace of life.

mammal most living things that belong to this special group have hair, give birth to live babies, and make milk to feed their babies.

paleontologist someone who studies very old life, such as dinosaurs, mostly by studying fossils.

prey an animal that is food for other animals.

tropical weather that is warm and wet.

INDEX